W9-CMI-368

Teaching English through the Arts

Teaching English through the Arts

R. Baird Shuman
University of Illinois at Urbana-Champaign

Denny Wolfe
Old Dominion University

National Council of Teachers of English
1111 Kenyon Road, Urbana, Illinois 61801

Staff Editor: Tim Bryant

Cover Design: Michael J. Getz

Interior Design: Tom Kovacs for TGK Design

NCTE Stock Number 50810-3020

Library of Congress Cataloging-in-Publication Data

Shuman, R. Baird (Robert Baird), 1929–
Teaching English through the arts / R. Baird Shuman, Denny Wolfe.
p. cm.
Includes bibliographical references.
ISBN 0-8141-5081-0
1. English language—Study and teaching (Secondary) 2. Arts—Study and teaching (Secondary) 3. Arts in literature. 4. Activity programs in education. I. Wolfe, Denny T. II. Title.
LB1631.S496 1990
428.4'071'2—dc20 90-37359
CIP

Contents

Introduction

While *Teaching English through the Arts* provides the necessary theoretical and historical basis for its fundamental approach, the book's major emphasis is on instructional strategies—twenty-nine of them—that classroom teachers who do not have special equipment, materials, or preparation in the arts can incorporate into their teaching. We have attempted in each suggested activity to consider the practical limitations and constraints within which many teachers work. Also in each activity, we suggest several learning outcomes that are likely to result from student participation.

We hope that both sections of this book—"Theory and Research" as well as "Practice"—will provide starting points for teachers who wish to extend or modify our approaches to meet their students' needs and aspirations. Even more ambitiously, we hope the book will help make secondary school English classrooms intensely exciting places for students and teachers alike. As individual teachers consider these ideas and activities for use in their own classes, they should feel free to choose and modify them according to their own preferences and those of their students. In fact, we would be surprised if teachers used and reused our suggestions without adaptation. We both welcome and encourage thoughtful adaptation of any material we have included, especially if the results of such changes prove even more beneficial for students.

Following a brief discussion of the theoretical and research-based support for our ideas, we present fifteen activities that focus on language, nine that focus on literature, and five that focus on writing. After careful consideration and after reviewing many current resources on teaching that are readily available to teachers, we decided to allow what might seem to some readers an imbalance in the number of activities devoted to each of the three strands we have chosen to treat. Obviously, we have included nearly twice as many activities for language as we have for literature, and three times as many for language as for writing. Our survey of the field led us to conclude that teachers can much more easily find fresh resources for teaching writing and literature than they can find for teaching language, particularly the elements of language that we have chosen to illustrate: dialects, usage and structure, semantics, and etymology. We trust that the fifteen activities we have suggested for teaching these various elements will both aid teachers and encourage them to find ways to incorporate more such emphases into their instructional plans.

Though not concerned specifically with using the arts to teach English, other Theory and Research Into Practice (TRIP) booklets of the National Council of Teachers of English are particularly useful to secondary school teachers looking for further ideas and help in the teaching of writing and literature. They include the following:

Writing

Richard Beach. *Writing about Ourselves and Others.*

Thom Hawkings. *Group Inquiry Techniques for Teaching Writing.*

Dawn and Raymond Rodrigues. *Teaching Writing with a Word Processor, Grades 7–13.*

William Strong. *Creative Approaches to Sentence Combining.*

Writing and Literature

Elizabeth Kahn, Carolyn Calhoun Walter, and Larry R. Johannesen. *Writing about Literature.*

Peter Smagorinsky, Tom McCann, and Stephen Kern. *Explorations: Introductory Activities for Literature and Composition, 7–12.*

In no way do we intend this book to be a substitute for comprehensive English textbooks and curriculum guides, nor for English teachers' own fertile imaginations. Rather, we intend it as a compact supplement—a "starter kit," if you will—that, when creatively adapted to specific situations, can help students make stimulating connections between English and some of the arts they know best—popular music, film, photography, design, drawing and painting, and drama. We hope and expect that our ideas and approaches will enable students—especially those whose greatest abilities sometimes lie outside the usual realm of English studies—to use the arts to increase their self-confidence as learners, to sharpen their sensibilities, and to improve their critical and creative thinking. If those hopes and expectations are indeed realized, everyone in the school community will certainly benefit.

1 Theory and Research

Historical Overview of the Language/Art Connection

As teachers, perhaps we can best appreciate the relationships between English and the arts if we consider the following four questions:

1. Why do we communicate in the forms we use?
2. How does oral communication differ from written communication?
3. What are the origins of written communication?
4. How have perceptions of such language processes as speaking and writing changed through the years—not merely the last couple of hundred, but through eons?

These questions, of course, are interrelated and must be answered accordingly.

In ancient societies, the art of writing had more to do with calligraphy and illumination than with the ways in which words were used to communicate information. In fact, information that people felt compelled to preserve was conveyed orally, through recitations of poems like *Beowulf* or *The Song of Roland,* or through songs, particularly ballads. If this literature was preserved at all in writing, it was artfully and laboriously recorded by scribes who were highly regarded in societies in which less than 1 percent of the populace was literate by conventional standards. The scribes preserved stories that grew out of their cultures, and the materials they produced were works of visual art.

Even earlier in human history, our ancestors left records in the form of pictures, like those preserved in the caves of Altamira or in the cliff dwellings of the Anasazi, who once inhabited what is now the southwestern United States. Documentation of human events and activities also exists in carvings on bones, stones, and other such artifacts that archeological digs all over the world continue to yield in profusion.

People in the farthest reaches of time obviously felt a need to record for posterity their activities, ideas, beliefs, and customs. Even today, people are perhaps motivated by primitive urges when they leave their marks on stone cliffs or tree trunks—or even on sidewalks and subway walls. Early people achieved many of their communicative ends through art, which in stylized forms eventually furnished the symbols from which ideographic writing was derived.

The stylized symbols of languages that came to be represented ideographically ultimately supplied the symbols from which alphabets grew. Consequently, the human race handed itself a great gift—a sophisticated and flexible means to construct a written form of language, using a limited number of symbols (twenty-six in English) in a nearly limitless number of combinations and permutations to produce a total word-hoard in English of almost 750,000.

For our purposes here, this brief overview leads to two pertinent conclusions:

1. Early composition that was used as a means of preserving and transmitting ideas and information through the ages took the forms of *songs* and *drawings.*
2. Early alphabetic writing was an art form that may have had less to do with composing the content of what was to be communicated than with the art form itself.

Obviously, connections between language and the arts have roots deep in antiquity. It is important now to consider learning itself—the epistemological roots of both language and art. These roots run equally deep.

What We Know and How We Know It

How do we know what we know? That is an intriguing question, indeed. We wish to deal with it here from its historical, philosophical, and psycholinguistic perspectives. Plato believed that the world we live in (i.e., the world of sensory experience) cannot be trusted. It fools us and tricks us and hinders our search for "truth." For him, people must discover truth through inexplicable, mystical leaps of insight—Eureka experiences, as it were.

Aristotle, Plato's student, believed with his teacher that the world of sensory experience indeed tricks us. But since it is all we have, he reasoned, we must use it. And if we are careful and prudent, Aristotle thought, we can learn by using general agreements among thinking people (or premises, if you will) as starting places in our search for specific truths. In other words, we can reason from *the general to the particular,* that is, deductive logic (e.g., "All men are mortal; Socrates is a man; ergo, Socrates is mortal").

Sir Francis Bacon believed that Aristotle had it backwards, that we learn by reasoning from *the particular to the general,* that is, inductive logic, or the modern scientific method (we observe, hypothesize, test, and then conclude). In the twentieth century, however, many who think about these matters—particularly linguists and psycholinguists—have been critical of the ancients' venerable views.

Modern thinkers have suggested that despite differences on many points, Plato, Aristotle, Bacon, and all who followed them shared one assumption in common: that knowledge is somewhere "out there" to be discovered. This assumption, modernists hold, is fundamentally wrong. In fact, they say, knowledge and truth exist in one place and in one place only: between a person's ears, i.e., "in here" rather than "out there" (Hayakawa 1941; Joos 1961; Smith 1971; Kelly 1955; Vygotsky 1962; Berthoff 1981). We *make* our meanings rather than absorb them. If we are to own our conceptual understanding, then, we must earn it. It is never a gift. It is a reward for arduous effort.

Several years ago, in a workshop we were conducting on writing across the curriculum, a teacher rose from her chair, placed her hands on her hips, and exclaimed, "This is fine, but I teach music. I'd like to see music taught across the curriculum, too. I think it's just as important as writing." This teacher said what others were thinking, so the proverbial cat was out of the bag. Another blurted, "Yeah, and what about art?"

Before things got completely out of hand, we said, "O.K., but let's talk about music first." The music teacher, in a somewhat calmer voice, pointed out that music was an early means of conveying history. Another observed that certainly music and poetry are connected (as in song lyrics) and that poetry set to music (ballads) was an early means of memorizing stories and passing them on from tribe to tribe—the so-called oral tradition. Yes, music has an interdisciplinary function, we agreed. A few hours later the workshop ended, and all of us went our separate ways.

A few days later, however, the two of us began talking seriously about what the music teacher had said in that workshop. One conclusion we reached was that, yes, it would be good to promote music across the curriculum—and, for that matter, sculpture, painting, photography, filmmaking, dance, acting, and design, as well. Why?

Because these arts are composing activities and—like talking and writing—powerful ways of making meaning.

Much has been made during the past two decades about "language for learning" (Emig 1978; Bruner 1969; Fulwiler 1982; Britton 1975; Berthoff 1981; Wolfe and Reising 1983), but the focus has been placed on verbal language only. It is time to realize that talking and writing are not powerful ways of learning simply because there is something inherently peculiar in these two language processes that makes them unique; on the contrary, *they are powerful ways of learning because they require people to deliver tangible evidence that thought has occurred and is occurring.* The vehicles for delivering this evidence are words strung together in sequences that carry meaning. But words are not the only vehicles for delivering such evidence. Musical compositions; sketches, drawings, and paintings; designs of various kinds; photographs; dramatic skits and improvisations; films—all of these provide other forms of evidence that thought has occurred and is occurring.

Some meaning-making activities provide more evidence of thinking and feeling than others do. For example, when we watch students read and listen, we cannot be sure that they are actively engaged in what they are doing; that is, while good readers and listeners are aggressive meaning-makers (just as talkers and writers are), their mental activities cannot literally be observed in the classroom. On the other hand, when we watch people write, draw, design, or otherwise compose, we have little doubt that their minds are busy and productive. We can literally observe that they are engaged in the processes of inventing and discovering—in other words, learning. Conceptual learning—the kind that endures and gives one power—is a composing, meaning-making activity.

Our own teaching experiences and those of others, together with sound learning theory, have made us aware that students need to handle the matter of learning in their own words (Ausubel 1968). But perhaps even that is too narrow a view of what is necessary for learning to occur. Certainly, one person's words may be expressed literally through conventional language; yet, another person's "words" may be expressed more figuratively as a painting, a musical composition, a photograph, a design, a film, perhaps even a cartoon. It is useful to think of "words" in the broadest sense as we draw connections between language and cognition.

Of course, few if any people are equally capable in all forms of artistic expression, but that observation is hardly the point. It is the galvanizing of thought through the use of any form of creative endeavor that contributes to learning; ideally, then, students should be permitted access to all of these composing, meaning-making processes. In a classroom where students are encouraged and permitted to use many different forms of composing and creating, the potential for learning seems greater than in classrooms where only limited forms are employed or allowed.

Human beings learn by *hand, eye, and brain* (Bruner 1969; Emig 1978); consequently, any learning process that simultaneously employs all three of these modes of learning is potent indeed. Reading, listening, and talking occur from the neck up; composing (writing, drawing, acting, designing, and the like) involves the whole person in the act of learning. It is for this reason that any overt composing activity is a powerful vehicle for both teaching and learning.

The process of doing/making, and the thinking it fosters, has been referred to as *operacy* (deBono 1976). While literacy (reading and writing) and oracy (talking and writing) are familiar goals and processes in any school's English curriculum, operacy has been sadly neglected. The irony of this situation is that both literacy and oracy can perhaps better be achieved by attending to operacy in our classrooms. Engaging students in processes that require them to create something enhances learning and facilitates achievement of the noblest goals of our curriculum.

What We Teach and How We Teach It

To what purposes we teach the elements of the English curriculum will always vary somewhat from school to school and from teacher to teacher. Each of us makes decisions nearly every day about the means and ends of dealing with the substance of our curriculum. However, we are not always conscious of what these means and ends are and of what the selection of them implies.

We can, for example, teach a short story in many different ways: as a work that contains ideas to illuminate thinking about a significant and current social issue; as a work with characters whose behavior inspires, comforts, disturbs, edifies, intrigues, confuses, or provokes; as a work with a theme that challenges established customs and values; and so on. On the other hand, our colleague in a room down the hall may teach the same short story to similar students on the same day as an example of abbreviated rising action, the use of flashback to minimize introductory information, limited denouement, or the use of an omniscient narrator.

Our point here is that we are all teaching English—we are teaching the short story—and we are shaping raw material into something that reflects our conceptions of what is important for students to learn. We can be content-centered, response-centered, elements-of-fiction-centered, or otherwise centered. The emphases we choose and the means by which we teach are informed by our philosophies, as well as by the philosophies of those who may have some control over our curriculum.

As another example, we may teach students about the English language either by prescribing for them the conventions of standard usage and forbidding in our classrooms the use of such expressions as "She don't," "I ain't," and "Me and her haven't went there yet" or by helping students understand the dynamics of a language that is ever-changing, ever-complex, and ever-growing—a language whose use varies in different geographical regions and in different social settings. Again, the focus we select and the means by which we teach largely depend upon the multifaceted and complicated contexts in which we live and work.

Many of us, serious though we are about teaching English, may genuinely disagree about what we teach and how we teach it. When called upon to do so, though, we can generally make our respective cases for the validity and rationality of most of our chosen emphases and approaches. Regardless of emphasis or approach, however, it is irrefutable that students tend to learn best when we stimulate their minds and channel their creative energies toward the shaping of concepts, the consideration of alternatives for decision making and problem solving, the making and understanding of metaphors, and the perceiving of connections between our discipline and others they study.

Further, students who learn to visualize as well as to listen, who discover that metaphoric thinking is ingrained in their daily lives and language (chairs have legs, needles and potatoes have eyes, ideas take flight), and who learn how to make meaning, gain the requisite intellectual and emotional equipment to function well in a democratic society. The world always needs aggressive makers and interpreters of meaning, solvers of problems, and thinkers of complex and coherent thoughts. Because the arts are composing processes, all of them can be employed to help students acquire these very desirable qualities.

How We Can Use the Arts as Pedagogy

"How can you tell a good painting from a bad one?" asks a character in Kurt Vonnegut's novel *Bluebeard.* The reply is "All you have to do, my dear, is look at a million paintings, and then you can never be mistaken" (p. 148). One part of the answer to how we can use the arts as pedagogy in the English classroom is simple: we must expose students to the arts, not just as consumers (viewers and listeners) but also as makers. Incorporating the arts into the English curriculum does not require us to rush to the nearest college or university to take courses in art, music, photography, filmmaking, dance, or dramatic improvisation (although to do so could lead to many rewarding experiences). Rather, we need to think through the inherent connections between art and the elements of English we teach.

Our students can learn quickly to forge links between English and the arts if they are given sufficient opportunities. To understand how these links develop, we might think about an art quite familiar to us as English teachers—writing. How do we define writing? Some of us might think of writing as "composition," the development of skill in forming concepts (i.e., making meaning) and of shaping them and recording them in some relatively lasting form. For those of us who hold this notion, writing has to do with invention, the outcomes of which constitute "literature," if we define the term broadly. A homely example of an act of writing that fulfills this definition might be something as literarily inconsequential as scribbling a note for one's spouse, child, or housemate and affixing it to the refrigerator door with a magnetized duck or apple. Such a note is not in the same league as a Shakespearean sonnet or an O'Neill play, but it is a member of the same broad family as the sonnet or the play, and, however humble, it has some literary form: sentences, clauses, phrases, punctuation, perhaps even paragraphing. And it has content, a "message"—i.e., a feeling, an idea, or a piece of information the writer wishes to convey.

Our point here is that writing is like all the other arts in this regard: all are composing activities and therefore require invention. Just as composition in speaking and writing has to do with ordering words, so composition in music has to do with ordering sound, and drawing or painting has to do with ordering objects in space, and so on. All forms of composition assist in the process of clarifying and ordering thought and feeling, in creating and understanding concepts—in short, in learning. All of us hope that our students will learn to think critically and creatively. But to do so, they must have practice. Involving students in the arts both ensures that practice and expands its variety.

If a person's notion of composing includes not only the mental activity of ordering ideas and feelings but also of setting down these ideas and feelings, then a major element of this process is the product itself—a painting, a musical score, a statue, a play, a film, a photograph, or the like. In writing, the process of physically creating such a product may be called handwriting or calligraphy. In any art, the process is whatever it takes to fix the ordered idea or captured feeling in some visible, tangible form. In music, this part of the composing process is notation; in the graphic arts it may be, say, clicking the shutter of the camera once the ordered images are arranged and set.

But to remain a moment longer with the process most familiar to us, the physical act of writing is in itself an art form, an extension of the drawing young children do as a necessary prelude to the letter formation and writing they will learn once their muscle development is sufficiently advanced to permit them to do the fine work that writing requires. (Consider also the ideographs of the oldest written languages, which included such items as a stylized picture of a house. The ideograph meant *house.* Eventually, the same ideograph came to represent the phoneme /b/, and as such could be used alphabetically to represent the *b* sound in all words that possessed that sound.)

The artistic antecedent of writing, then, is drawing; the artistic antecedents of literature are songs, oral stories, improvisations, and other informal means of "acting out." Given these artistic antecedents and their history stretching through eons, it seems clear that the collective unconscious of human beings is rooted in artistic archetypes. John Barrie (1986) suggests as much in his interpretation of the Swiss psychologist Carl Jung: "In relation to Jungian theory, an important emphasis is that art is the expression of universal mythic content emanating from the deep substrata of the collective unconscious mind" (p. 43). English teachers who are aware of these archetypes and who find ways to tie their teaching to them will likely open learning possibilities for students that might otherwise remain closed. To state our case more precisely, the unconscious has a role to play in human learning processes, and as we invite students in our English classes to compose in various art forms (in addition to writing), we simultaneously offer them new and fertile strategies to enhance their learning.

Conclusion

In the act of viewing a work of art (such as a painting or a film), or listening to one (such as a musical composition), or reading one (such as a poem), students must be led to engage in language/learning processes actively rather than passively. In his book *The Courage to Create,* Rollo May (1975) connects the acts of making art and consuming it by calling them both creative processes; and he implicitly expresses a hope that all English teachers have for their students:

> In our appreciation of the created work—say a Mozart quintet—we also are performing a creative act. When we engage a painting, which we have to do especially with modern art if we are authentically to see it, we are experiencing some new moment of sensibility. Some new vision is triggered in us by our contact with the painting; something unique is born in us. This is why appreciation of the music or painting or other works of the creative person is also a creative act on our part. (pp. 15–16)

In order to help students arrive at a developmental stage of growth in which they can genuinely appreciate art (e.g., literature, drama, sculpture), we can expose them to it in its many forms. It is also important to acknowledge that empathy is necessary for appreciating and experiencing what May calls a "new moment of sensibility." What more practical and potentially better way of helping students both gain a sense of empathy and heighten their sensibilities than by engaging them in composing activities through many art forms? When we do that, students become increasingly able and sophisticated consumers of art, users of language, and thinkers of elevated, complex thoughts.

Throughout America, virtually every school division's English curriculum guide expresses at least three common goals. We are to help students (1) distinguish between literal and figurative meaning; (2) become lifelong readers, writers, and critical thinkers; and (3) develop a sense of aesthetic appreciation. Using all the arts as teaching strategies to accomplish these goals is both a desirable practice and an exciting prospect. Clearly, in the hands of willing and energetic teachers, the arts can be used—at the least—to motivate students' interests in the substance and processes of English. Further, teachers in most areas of teaching can do much to heighten students' artistic awareness in natural ways and can, as well, help students achieve legitimate instructional goals. Remarkably, in doing this, all of us can enable our students to learn in new ways, to learn more effectively and lastingly than they might have before, and to tap the archetypal patterns of knowing that we all possess.

2 Practice

Language

In this section, we illustrate the following elements of language: dialects, usage and structure, semantics, and etymology.

Dialects

The study of dialects is an often neglected feature of the English curriculum. Yet it is a subject that intrigues students. Many teachers have found that engaging students in the study of dialects builds interest in Standard American English—itself merely a dialect, albeit the "power language" of our society.

Using Design as a Conceptual Basis for Teaching Dialectal Differences

Ask students to consider how the structure of the word *dialect* is like a three-story building. Elicit as many responses as possible. If no one else observes that the word has three syllables, point out that fact.

Now ask students to visualize various houses or buildings that surround the places where they live. Organize the class into pairs in which individuals will describe to each other the different features their selected houses or buildings possess. As an out-of-class assignment, ask students to identify houses or buildings around their homes that seem the most different from each other and to list the differences in as much detail as possible. During class, ask students, in pairs again, to share their lists. Point out to students that the lists they have created and discussed were based upon visualizing.

Now say that you would like to test their powers of listening. Play a tape of any two dialects that you have available—perhaps two dialects you have recorded from the surrounding community. Afterwards, ask students to list any differences between the two dialects they heard. Ask them to pair off again and share their lists. In whole-class discussion, ask students to say whether or not they heard in either of the two recorded dialects any language features that would not be acceptable in the dialect generally designated as Standard American English. Help students see that the social context for language usage—much like architectural styles and structures in particular locales—determines whether or not a given dialect usage is acceptable or unacceptable.

This activity helps students:

- develop powers of visualizing and listening
- compare and contrast dialectal differences
- analyze the role of social context in determining the acceptability of dialects

Using Music to Teach Pronunciation and Diction

Pronunciation and diction (word choice) are features of dialect study that students find both interesting and entertaining to investigate. Song lyrics provide one fertile source for analyzing these features.

Offer these five categories of music:

country/western
hard rock
soft rock
pop rock
rap

Divide the class into groups of four or five students each. Ask each group to select one category of music, one artist within that category, and one song by that artist. Each group chooses one person to bring to class a written copy of the selected song lyrics. Another person is chosen to read the song lyrics aloud. As group members hear the lyrics read, they jot down words and phrases they believe are pronounced and/or used in a dialect other than Standard American English. Group members share their lists and consolidate their words and phrases into one list, according to the consensus of the group. Each group then "translates" their listed words and phrases into Standard American English, with a recorder transcribing the modified lyrics. Then each oral reader shares his or her group's rendering of the song lyrics in the dialect of Standard American English.

This activity helps students:

- practice active listening
- appreciate dialectal differentiation
- acquire a sense of the importance of pronunciation and diction in conveying meaning through the various rhythms of language

Writing, Acting, and Drawing for Understanding Figurative Language

Remind students of such idioms as "keep your nose to the grindstone," "flying off the handle," "blowing your top," "their eyes lit up," and "that's a load off my mind." Now ask them to give examples of figurative statements from any familiar dialect of English.

Ask them to either explain in writing the difference between the figurative and literal meanings of their examples, do an improvisation that depicts the literal meaning of each example (working with one or more other students), or make a drawing or some other artistic representation of what each idiom means literally. (If your students have access to computers, encourage them to create graphic designs that illustrate their idioms. Collages also work well with this lesson.)

This activity helps students:

- distinguish between literal and figurative language
- visualize some of the humorous aspects of their language
- invent new ways of expressing themselves

Role Playing to Establish the Place of Standard American English

Ask students to consider the following proposition: "While our personal *idiolects* (the speech patterns unique to each individual speaker) and *dialects* (the speech patterns characteristic of a region or a particular community of speakers) certainly have their place, everyone should learn to use Standard American English when it is called for in a speaking situation."

Now ask students to divide into groups of four or five. Each group should create a list of reasons to establish the validity of the above proposition. A minimum of three reasons is required. Each of these three (or more) reasons must be written in Standard English for review by the teacher. Individual groups elect two students to represent their group before the whole class (a total of perhaps five or six pairs of students). One of these students will play the role of television interviewer, and the other will play the role of an interviewee who is an expert linguist. In the course of a five-minute interview, the interviewee must defend the proposition by giving three reasons that his or her group created. After the interview, the class offers opinions by a show of hands as to whether the interviewee did indeed give three distinct and valid reasons in support of the proposition. The group represented by the interviewee says whether the class was right or wrong in its majority opinion. After the interviews, ask the class to indicate which interviewees and which reasons seemed to support the proposition most convincingly, and why.

This activity helps students:

- consider the merits of learning Standard American English
- value linguistic diversity
- practice persuasive rhetorical techniques

Usage and Structure

If students are to master Standard American English, they must be able to employ the conventions and customs of language expression in that dialect; however, attempts to learn these conventions through drill exercises in textbooks and workbooks often prove boring and uninspiring. Also, studying usage and structure outside the context of what one intends to *do* with language seems pointless to students. Language study will become more interesting and productive if we employ the arts as teaching strategies.

Pop Art as an Aid to Teaching Usage

Ask students to select cartoons from a daily newspaper (preferably a Sunday edition) which contain usage problems, such as *between* vs. *among; ain't* for *am not, are not, is not, has not,* or *have not; who* vs. *whom; nohow* for *in no way; few* vs. *less; don't* vs. *doesn't; none* vs. *any; was* vs. *were; saw* vs. *seen; did* vs. *done.* If students have difficulty finding cartoons with usage errors, tell them to create their own. Ask them to bring their cartoons to class and to find one or more partners with whom to rehearse a performance of their cartoons for the whole class. As each cartoon is performed for the class, students try to identify and correct the usage errors they hear. Keep a record of the usage errors students illustrate through their selected cartoons. Near the end of the class, choose a few errors that you want the whole class to take particular note of. Give examples of the errors within the context of complete sentences, and ask the class to respond in chorus to correct the errors. (For example, "I ain't a crook." Class responds, "I am not a crook.")

This activity helps students:

- understand the concept of *usage* as a linguistic term
- identify some common usage problems in English
- demonstrate ability to correct common usage problems

Films and Television as Texts for Mastering Subject-Verb Agreement

Organize students into groups of four or five. Ask the groups to list their currently favorite films or television shows. Each group then selects one film or television show that each group member is at least somewhat familiar with. They should try to identify a character from their selected film or television show who might be most likely to commit errors in subject-verb agreement. Some possibilities might include Carla from the television sitcom "Cheers," Tom Cruise's character in the film *Rain Man,* or Wild Thing from the film *Major League.* In subgroups of two or three, students write short dialogues between their selected characters and someone else. In the dialogues, their characters should commit at least one error in subject-verb agreement. (Students may consult their grammar handbooks for examples of errors.) Subgroups read their dialogues to their other group partners, and the group chooses one of these dialogues for reading to the whole class, which identifies and corrects errors in subject-verb agreement. Keep a record of the examples students use in the dialogues. Select a few subject-verb agreement errors that you want the whole class to pay particular attention to. Near the end of the class, share your list with everyone.

This activity helps students:

- clarify their understanding of subject-verb agreement
- collaborate on solving subject-verb agreement problems
- monitor their own progress toward mastering subject-verb agreement in Standard English usage

Throwing the Body into Sentence Formation

Find out what books your students are having trouble understanding in one or more of their other classes. Get copies of the books they are agonizing over. Look through them and select some quite difficult sentences of at least ten words but no more than fifteen. On sheets of paper or on uniform pieces of cardboard, copy with a black magic marker the words that make up the sentence, one word to a card. Make sure not to leave out any words. Capitalize only proper nouns. Include no marks of punctuation other than hyphens and apostrophes.

As your students file into the classroom, give one card to each student until you have distributed the set for one sentence. Once the class is seated, say, "Everyone with a card come to the front of the room." When they have done so, say, "Make yourselves into an acceptable English sentence. Everyone who has a card *must* be included in the sentence." It should take less than a minute for your students, working together, to form a sentence. Ask a student who is using the book from which the sentence was taken to read the sentence and then to compare it to the sentence in the book from which it came.

As an additional activity, let your students work with a short list of words, perhaps seven or eight, that make up a sentence when put together properly. When they have structured themselves into a sentence, ask them if what they have is really a sentence. They will soon agree that it is. Then say, "If you have something that's whole and complete, and add something to it, is it still whole and complete?" Some of them will probably answer affirmatively. Then produce one more card, this one with a word like *when, although,* or *otherwise* on it, and ask a student to join the sentence the other students have produced. As soon as the subordinating conjunction becomes part of the sentence, most students will realize that the whole, complete sentence they have just identified is now neither whole nor complete. A lesson in subordination, a topic some students find confusing, is thus taught visually, kinesthetically, and dramatically.

This activity helps students:

- build sophisticated sentences
- *see* rather than read about how sentences are constructed
- come to an understanding of subordination and other grammatical conventions

Artistic Options for Pronoun-Antecedent Agreement

Tell students that they can exempt an assignment or test, or that they can earn extra points, if they choose to draw, sketch, or paint to your satisfaction illustrations of the following rules:

1. Pronouns should agree in number with their antecedents. For example:
   Many of the players began to doubt their abilities.
   One of the boys began to doubt his ability.
2. Two or more antecedents connected by *and* must be referred to by a plural pronoun. For example:
   Mitchell and Ashley have completed their exams.
3. Two or more singular antecedents joined by *or* or *nor* must be referred to by a singular pronoun. For example:
   Either the coach or the principal has to give some of her time to charity.

4. If one of two antecedents joined by *or* or *nor* is singular and one is plural, the pronoun must agree with the nearer antecedent. For example:

   Either the principal or the coaches have to give some of their time to charity.

Review the submitted drawings, sketches, and/or paintings, checking them for clarity, accuracy, and general quality. Perhaps after recommending some revisions, place one, some, or all of the products on a wall in the classroom. Occasionally, use class time to point to the illustrations on the wall and ask for sentences to illustrate the rule(s). For particularly good sentences, offer the student(s) who supplied them additional credit for matching their sentences with the illustrations on the wall.

This activity helps students:

- use their particular talents to demonstrate understanding of rules that govern pronoun-antecedent agreement
- maintain a consciousness of rules that govern pronoun-antecedent agreement
- generate varieties of examples to illustrate the rules

Semantics

With and through language, human beings perceive, portray, and shape their realities. As people grow in their powers to use and to interpret language, they also grow in their powers to control and to comprehend their environment. Through semantic studies (inquiries into the nuances and varieties of meanings that language conveys), students can develop their abilities to use and to interpret language in increasingly sophisticated ways.

Illustrating Our Semantic Environment

Begin with a discussion of the meanings of *figurative* language and *literal* language. See if your class can distinguish between the two terms. Help as necessary. Then give students the statements in the list below. Ask them to take photographs, make drawings, or cut out pictures from magazines and/or newspapers to convey both the figurative and literal meanings each statement carries. Each student can select one or more statements to illustrate, as you choose.

The ice is hot.

Jack is one bad dude.

"I wish to toast the entire team," the president said.

Mel's speech was full of holes and throwaway lines.

It appears that the senator is trying another end run.

"I can't find my prepared remarks, so I'll just have to wing it," the speaker said.

"I'm history," Bill said, as he ran out of the dining room.

The program had bugs in it.

"Don't rain on my parade," Michelle told Sonny.

"Let's put Tom's motion back on the table," the chairperson said.

Collect students' materials—their photographs, their sketches, or their cut-out pictures. If you have two classes engaged in this project, distribute each class's products to the other. (Put numbers on each student's contribution rather than the student's name.) Divide students into groups of four or five. Each student in the group interprets to other group members the double messages his or her pictures convey. Group members extend or correct individual interpretations. Finally, each group selects its favorite contribution—one per group—to be shared with everyone and/or displayed in the classroom. Try to have each of the ten sentences represented, if possible.

This activity helps students:

- distinguish between the terms *literal* and *figurative*
- interpret language with dual or multiple meanings
- practice metaphorical thinking

Advertising and Semantic Pollution

Point out to students that a large part of our semantic environment is occupied by advertising—on billboards, on television, in magazines and newspapers. Also point out that much of this advertising is aimed toward manipulating our thinking, modifying our values, and controlling our behavior—all for the purpose of peddling products. Use as an illustration certain billboard ads for cigarettes, showing healthy, attractive young men and women in exotic locations, doing exciting or relaxing things—despite the fact that cigarette smoking is generally conceded to be damaging to one's health.

Also use the following Hilton ad that has frequently appeared in *Life* and other contemporary magazines:

> Now the whole country is open for exploration. From star-watching in Hollywood to show stopping in New York City.

From Dixieland jazz in New Orleans to a symphony in Boston. Just stay with Hilton. And the country is yours in one attractive, bargain-priced package.

Ask students if they can think of other examples. As students offer them, involve the whole class in analyzing the ads. Ask, "What exactly is the ad saying? What is it conveying that it does not say directly?"

Divide students into pairs. Ask the pairs to decide on a product that they might be able to write an ad for—one like the ads you've discussed. But rather than writing an ad to be *read,* the pairs should write one to be *sung.* When the pairs have finished their work, organize the class into groups of three pairs each. Each group will select one ad from the three possibilities. The selected ad will be rehearsed and sung to the entire class. If possible, have any musicians in the class serve as resources to the groups, giving advice and perhaps playing instruments to accompany the group singing. After each group performance, analyze the ad in whole-class discussion. The crucial question every time is "What is the ad really saying and selling?"

This activity helps students:

- consider critically the language of advertising
- analyze advertisements to determine their subtle messages
- become selective and rational consumers

A Semantic Look at the Classics through Creative Dramatics

Show students the following titles:

Gone with the Wind
The Scarlet Letter
Rear Window
A Farewell to Arms
Somebody Up There Likes Me

Tell them a little about the significance of each title. *Gone with the Wind,* in one sense, signifies the death of the Old South; *The Scarlet Letter* is the red letter *A* worn by Hester Prynne to denote her adultery; *Rear Window* refers to the back window of an apartment through which a homebound photographer witnesses a murder; *A Farewell to Arms* refers both to the leaving of love and the leaving of war; and *Somebody Up There Likes Me* refers to a boxer's faith in the Almighty.

Now ask students to invent other possible points of significance for these titles. *Gone with the Wind* might suggest some interesting and clever possibilities if *wind* is pronounced as "Wind the watch"; *The Scarlet Letter* might refer to the sort of thing one writes to a lover, rather than to the beginning of the alphabet; and so on.

Divide the students into groups of four or five and ask them to prepare short skits to portray imaginative/absurd/witty/believable—in short, different and offbeat—interpretations of these titles. (Students may select other titles, if they choose.) Allow each group to perform its skit for the whole class. (Some groups may rather wish merely to describe their skits than perform them. Permit that option, if you think it is necessary.) Use these skits as one way to help students discover differences between literal and figurative language.

This activity helps students:

- develop a sense of the playful possibilities of semantic inquiry
- think inventively and interpretively
- distinguish between literal and figurative language

Etymology

"Words," Lewis Thomas wrote, "are the cells of language, moving the great body on legs" (1978, p. 135). As cells are the structural units of plant and animal life, so words are the structural units of language. Students' first fascination with language can begin with etymological studies, i.e., inquiries into the histories of words. A good resource for these studies is *The Oxford English Dictionary,* or *OED,* which may be purchased by school libraries—with a magnifying glass—for less than two hundred dollars per two-volume set.

Sketching Word Origins

Write the word *hieroglyphic* on the chalkboard and ask students to say what it means. What you wish to emphasize is that pictures, as symbolic representations of letters, words, feelings, and ideas, were a primitive form of written language and the origin of recorded history. Through class discussion, find out what exposure students have had to hieroglyphics. (They may talk about having seen magazine pictures of drawings on the walls of ancient caves, television documentaries about prehistoric time periods, museum pieces, and so on.)

Now point out that many words have interesting origins in English. For example, the word *influence* was once used mainly as an astrological term to denote an ethereal fluid from the stars that penetrates a baby's body at birth and determines its destiny. Ask students to describe how they might portray that meaning as a picture. (Try your hand at drawing on the chalkboard. You might draw a star, with some curved lines coming down from it to enter the bedroom window of a house.)

Write the following words on the chalkboard (or you may prefer to use your own): *tattle, fluster, cursor, blizzard,* and *pamper.* Ask students to say what each word means in its most contemporary sense. They will probably note that *tattle* means "to tell on someone" (used primarily by children); *fluster,* "to become confused or upset"; *cursor,* "the marker on a computer screen, used in word processing"; *blizzard,* "a snowstorm"; and *pamper,* "to spoil, to coddle, or to indulge someone."

Now divide the class into five groups, giving each group a card with one word on it. In addition to the word, the card will have on it indications of what century the word first appeared in English and its initial meaning, as follows: *tattle* (15th c.), to gossip or to chatter; *fluster* (15th c.), to excite with intoxicating drink; *cursor* (14th c.), a runner who carries messages; *blizzard* (19th c.), a riddle; *pamper* (14th c.), to cram with food, to feed luxuriously. Ask each group to review the original definition of its assigned word. Each individual in the group should try to produce a sketch that illustrates the word's original meaning. Group members select the one that will represent the whole group. As each group shows the class its selected sketch, the class tries to guess the word's meaning, then which word the sketch has portrayed. For example, the group with *tattle* might have drawn three individuals seated together, all talking at the same time. The class might say, "This word means *talking at once.*" (They probably will have to decide between *tattle* and *fluster* in this instance, given the two words' contemporary meanings and the sketch they are using as a basis for their guesses.) After each group has presented its sketch, all five sketches could be displayed on classroom walls. Using the *OED,* students could explore other word histories for similar discussions and/or displays.

This activity helps students:

- recognize the etymological features of words
- infer meanings from graphic symbols of verbal language
- discover why words carry multiple meanings

Designing Etymological Charts

As students rummage around in books like the *OED* and standard English dictionaries, they notice how words and accompanying information are ordered and arranged. Lead a class discussion about what students can recall from their experiences with such reference works. Ask questions like "What can you discover about a word by looking it up in the *OED*? In your desk dictionary? How is all this information about words organized?"

After class discussion, divide students into small groups. Ask the groups to examine dictionaries and/or the *OED* and make a list to show, in order, all of the different types of information offered about any given word. Then ask the groups to create a design (or chart) that would most creatively, efficiently, and attractively display all the information that major reference sources give about words. Ask the groups to decide whether they would delete or add any information about words they find in their reference sources. After each group has worked out its design, it should choose a word to illustrate how its design actually looks. Each group should illustrate its prototype. Among all the groups' designs, the class might determine the one it likes best for display on a classroom bulletin board.

This activity helps students:

- develop proficiency in using standard reference materials
- organize and categorize information about the history of language
- create and evaluate alternative ways of displaying information

Drama and Drawing to Learn Mythological Origins of Words

Ask students to give examples of words and phrases they routinely hear that have their origins in sports. (You might give the word *catch,* as in "Catch my meaning?" as an example, or "He threw us a curve on that test!") Now ask them to say whether they know any words—even any stories or characters (e.g., Orion, Pegasus, Ulysses)—that might have roots in Greek and Roman mythology but that also have modern significance. (While students will have more difficulty with this question, they will soon realize how their limited knowledge of mythology can constrain their understanding of modern language.)

Divide students into five groups. Give each group a pair of words, written individually on 3 × 5 index cards, as follows: *tantalize, erotic; fury, epicurean; thespian, phoenix; siren, grace; lunatic, narcissism.* Tell the groups that they should look up their two words in the *OED* or their dictionaries (either will suffice for this activity). What they are to do is find the mythological origins of their words.

Next, they should prepare to present one of the two words to the class either by drawing a representation of it on the chalkboard or by dramatically illustrating it without talking. Tell them that every group member must be involved in either the drawing or the drama. Their representation of the word must be drawn from its mythological origin. (For example, *tantalize* might be dramatically illustrated by one group member—Tantalus—being "teased" by other group members.) The class must guess the word each group is representing. If the class guesses a group's word, the successful group gets to present its second word immediately, but in the mode other than the one they used before. (One object of this activity is to see which group or groups can present both words and have the class correctly guess the words. Eventually, however, each group should have an opportunity to represent both words to the class.)

After all groups have presented their words, conduct a whole-class review to be sure that everyone understands the meanings of all ten words.

This activity helps students:

- perceive the importance of language history to the shaping of modern meaning
- discover the mythological roots of many modern words
- increase their vocabularies

From Pictures to Words and Back Again: An Introductory Lesson

Tell students that the writing system most of us are used to is a relative latecomer in the history of human existence. The earliest forms of writing were actually artwork—pictures on the walls of caves, messages etched on the smooth inside bark of trees, carvings from animal bones. The only problem with these forms of writing was that such important subtleties as verb tense and the attribution of abstract qualities were difficult to communicate in them.

Through the years, therefore, drawing became increasingly stylized, and finally stylized depictions of physical objects were appropriated as letters of the alphabet that, in combination with other letters, formed words. The letter *A,* for example, originally represented the horns of an animal like an ox. Through the centuries, its representation came to look less and less like the horns of oxen, eventually so much so that *A* began to have a life of its own detached from its historical origins in pictographic writing (writing that communicates through pictures, sometimes called *hieroglyphs*). See Fig. 1.

It is said that everything comes full circle, and such has been the case with pictographic writing. As society has become increasingly multinational, it has become necessary, particularly in areas frequented by foreigners, to communicate basic, necessary information through

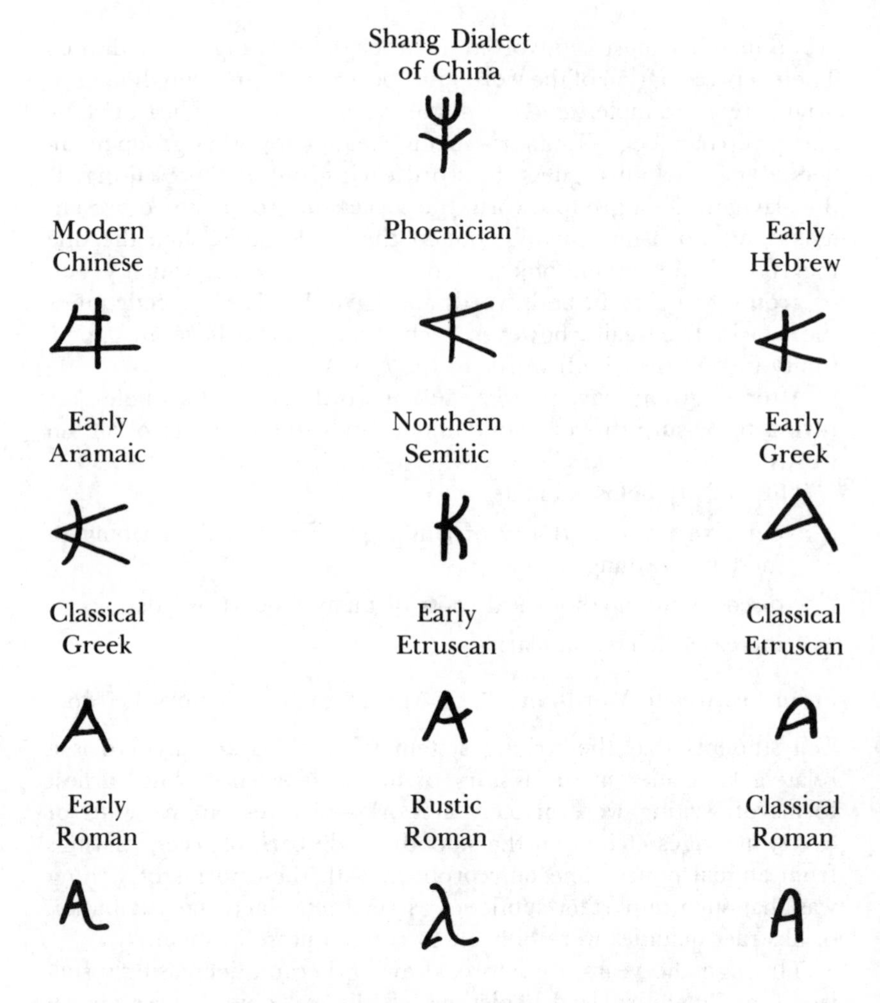

Figure 1. The evolution through various languages of the Roman letter *A*, which is used in English, from an early Chinese (Shang) pictograph that depicts *ox*.

pictures, sometimes stylized, that relay a message that is not dependent upon one's ability to speak a given language. Speakers of English, German, Dutch, French, Chinese, Bantu, Arabic, and Icelandic can all tell which restroom door to enter if one door bears the picture of a figure in a skirt, the other a picture of a figure in trousers. One does not have to know any particular one of the world's more than a thousand languages to know that a skull and crossbones on a bottle is a warning that it contains something poisonous. The skull and crossbones is an international sign.

This lesson consists of two parts, each to be broached on different, not necessarily consecutive, days. The first day will be devoted to reviewing in class drawings or pictures of various pictographs students have found and brought to class after a day or two of looking. They might copy some of the common road signs they see, take pictures of them, or make photocopies of pictographs they find in books or magazines. Hundreds of such pictographs surround us. Students might find some of them in such sources as the study manual for a driver's license, but this source is only a tiny corner of the huge field of possibilities.

As students show their pictographs, encourage members of the class to identify each depiction in writing, indicating what it is about each pictograph that reveals its meaning. Do any two or more different pictographs communicate the same message? Does one communicate it better than another, or are both equally clear in what is being communicated? Help students to see that different sentences, like different pictographs, can communicate the same things, but that style, tone, emphasis, sequence of ideas, and other crucial elements enter into the basic impact each sentence makes.

The second part of this exercise can be done by students singly or working in pairs or groups. The task is to identify some area in which pictographs might be useful but have apparently not yet been used. For example, a pictograph might be used instead of the sign "10 Items or Less" at the express checkout register in a supermarket.

Students need to devise situations and then work to meet the need to communicate something about each situation. They should do this by explaining in writing—not more than a sentence or two—exactly what they want to say. Once they have committed their messages into pictographs, they need to write an explanation of how they think each one communicates. All the students or groups of students will present their pictographs to the class and invite their fellow students to write down the message the pictograph communicates. They then give the message from which they worked to create each pictograph.

This activity helps students:

- learn something about the history of writing
- know in what ways writing is a direct outgrowth of the graphic arts
- translate a pictographic message into a written one and vice versa

Literature

Literature is the tangible content (some would say "meat") of any school's English curriculum—literature in its many forms: poems, plays, short stories, novels, films, essays, cartoons. Through studying literature, many students become better speakers, listeners, readers, writers, observers, and thinkers. Our loftiest goals are that students will use literature throughout their lives as a source for growth in both language and thought, and that they will gradually come to appreciate literature as art. One way to help students approach these goals is to use the other arts as vehicles for teaching and learning.

Using Song Lyrics and a Famous Poem to Compare Tragic Figures

Ask students what makes a "tragic figure." Along with other characteristics you and your students might mention, be sure to cite two qualities in particular: (1) tragic figures always seem larger than life; (2) despite their many admirable characteristics, tragic figures always have some flaw that brings about their demise or downfall. Tell students you would like them to compare the characteristics of an actual person and a fictional person to determine whether (and how) each might be viewed as a tragic figure.

Now play Elton John's song "Candle in the Wind," about the life and legend of the Hollywood film star Marilyn Monroe. As they listen, students should jot down any words they hear that hint of Marilyn's qualifications as a tragic figure (at least as the song portrays her). After students listen to the song, ask the following questions: Do you think the singer portrays Marilyn as a tragic figure? Why or why not? From the song, what sort of picture do you get of Marilyn? How does the singer suggest that Marilyn is like a candle? Does this image "work" for you as a listener? Why or why not?

Now introduce students to Edwin Arlington Robinson's poem "Richard Cory." (You might play a recording of Simon and Garfunkel's song about Richard.) Read the poem aloud, or ask a student to read it aloud. (Be sure it's read well.) Ask students to listen for any hints of Richard's qualifications as a tragic figure and to take any notes that they think are useful for discussion afterward. When the reading is over, ask the following questions: Do you think the poet portrays Richard as a tragic figure? Why or why not? From the poem, what sort of picture do you get of Richard? How does the poet suggest that Richard is like a king? Does this image work for you as a reader? Why or why not? In what ways do you see Marilyn Monroe and Richard Cory as having similar qualities and characteristics? In what ways do you see the two as different?

This activity helps students:

- perceive the rhythmical qualities of poetry and songs
- determine what makes a "tragic figure"
- compare and contrast character traits

Using Drama and Design to Introduce the Theme of Urban versus Rural Life

Ask students to stand beside their desks and close their eyes. Direct them as follows:

> Imagine you're walking down a busy city sidewalk on a hot summer day in the afternoon. Imagine what you might see around you, what you might hear, smell, and even taste. Colors? Odors? Sounds? Concentrate. I'll be quiet for a minute.
>
> Imagine that in front of you on the sidewalk is a stick. You pick it up. To the left of the sidewalk is an iron railing that goes on for blocks. You hold the stick by one end and you run the other end along the railing as you walk. How does it sound? Make you feel? Off to the left of the sidewalk, you see a gutter drain—an iron grating. There's something shiny inside this drain. You look closer. It's a silver dollar! You drop to one knee and reach in. You stretch, stretch, stretch. Did you get it? Open your eyes.
>
> ——————— [pause] ———————
>
> Now close your eyes again, and forget that city place. Imagine you're walking down a dusty country road on a hot summer's day, in the late morning. Look to the sky. What do you see there? Is it clear and blue, or are there clouds? What do you hear? Perhaps birds chirping. There are no sounds of the city in this place. Often it's quiet here. How does the silence sound? I'll be quiet a moment.
>
> Off to the left you hear the sound of a running stream. You'd like to get to that place. To do so you'll have to leave the road and walk through high grass. As you walk through this grass, it touches your skin—your arms and your face. Does it scratch? Imagine how it feels. Suddenly you find yourself standing under a huge oak tree beside a brook. You look down, and at your feet you see a bamboo pole with a string tied around one end, evidence of a young fisherman's having been there. Open your eyes. Sit down.
>
> At your seats, make a list of all the images, sounds, odors, and other sensory experiences you can remember from your first walk down the city sidewalk. Don't make these up, now! Write down only what you honestly remember.
>
> ——————— [pause] ———————

Now make a list of all the sensory experiences you can remember from your walk down the dusty country road.

Swap your list with a partner. When you read your partner's list, see if you can guess which place he or she prefers—the city place or the country place.

———————— [pause] ————————

How many of you guessed correctly? Now, write one sentence that says which place you prefer, and why—the city or the country.

———————— [pause] ————————

Who's willing to read what they wrote?

———————— [pause] ————————

I'm going to read a poem to you. But before I do, what do you think this poem is about, based on what we've been doing?

As you hear this poem read aloud, try to identify who "they" are. [At this point, read "Citykid."]

Citykid

They took the boy out of the city
But no matter how they tried
They could not wrest the city magic
From the boy.

He looked at trees and rushing streams
And in them saw reminders of light posts
And teams of people flooding into subway stops
At half past five.

They told him he must walk in woods through autumn gold,
That he must learn to hunt and fish to be a man
But he had hunted, fished for coins through gratings
And walked in autumn woods at ten or twelve
When people prowl the streets to make seductions,
When eyes peer in the darkness avidly like Rousseau's tigers*
And hands stroke body parts bound tight in clothes.

The boy was made to feel he was wrong
And they were right.
For, with them, there was no middle ground,
Just right and those who did not fit its mold:
The boy, enduring now in their good hands
The punishment, the soul starvation
of a rehabilitation
Out of town.

— R. Baird Shuman

* Rousseau's tigers: French painter Henri Rousseau, most famous of the "primitive" painters recognized by modern art history.

After reading the poem aloud, ask students to say who "they" are. (Although the poet never precisely identifies "them," we can assume "they" are adult authority figures who have power over the boy, and who—perhaps mistakenly—think they know better than the boy what's best for him.)

Divide students into groups; ask each group to create a design for the poem that suggests essentially what the poem is about. In other words, each group should create a drawing or a sketch to illustrate the poem in some way. Figure 2 is a simple example. (In this drawing, we are trying to depict an implicit question in the poem: is the city or the country better for the boy? Also, we have drawn our "road sign" in the general shape of the poem.)

Ask each group to show its design to the class, and to comment on what the design is intended to convey. If you wish, place all designs on the walls of your classroom.

Lead a class discussion of the poem. You might particularly wish to ask, "Do you find any irony in the poem? If so, where?" (Note particularly the last four lines.)

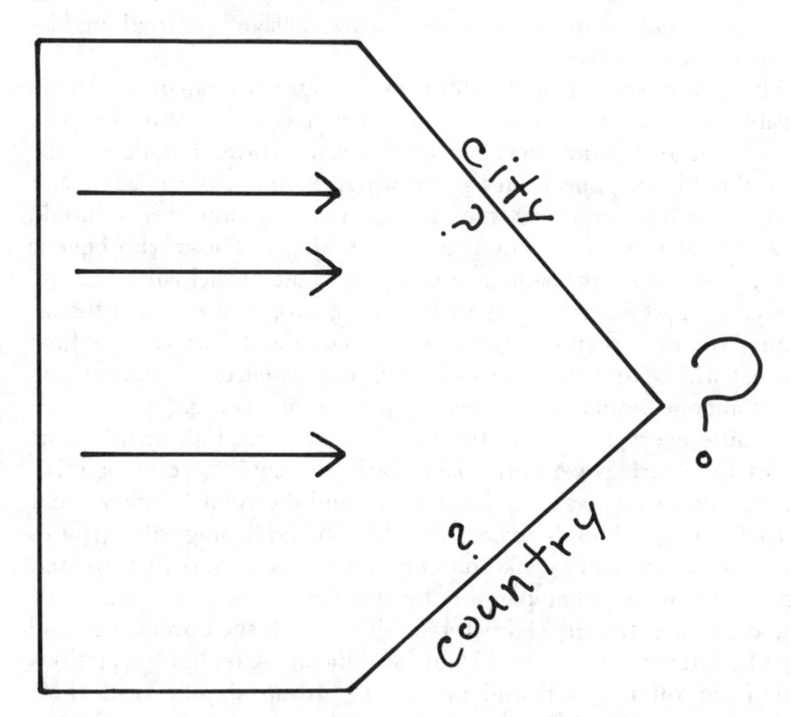

Figure 2. A graphic representation of the poem "Citykid," suggesting the directions the poem is taking and the issue with which it deals.

You might now wish to go on to other literature that portrays city (urban) and country (rural) life, values, and/or issues. A few possibilities are such familiar poems as Sandburg's "Fog" and "Chicago," Wordsworth's "The World Is Too Much with Us"; a play, Saroyan's *The Oyster and the Pearl;* a nonfiction book, Thoreau's *Walden;* and novels, Sue Ellen Bridger's *All Together Now* and Harper Lee's *To Kill a Mockingbird.*

This activity helps students:

- note the organizational symmetry of a poem
- compare and contrast urban life and rural life
- expand their understanding of irony as a literary concept

Visualizing—Part 1: Characterization and Situation

After a group of students has read six to eight short stories, divide them into groups of about five. Each group will be responsible for one of the short stories. Its task will be to make suitable covers for the short stories as if each were to be bound separately as a booklet. The covers may be drawings, water colors, collages, or anything else the groups can devise.

The covers should be as literal as the students can make them, possibly depicting one or two of the characters in the story in some sort of crucial situation that helps the plot to evolve. The title of the story should not appear on the drawing, painting, or collage. (Not all students have equal artistic ability, so each group ideally should have in it at least one student with such ability. Those who believe they cannot draw or paint are still important participants because they can supply ideas and guidance as the project proceeds.) Just as writing requires revision, the changes required to arrive at a final product will be arrived at through revision, albeit of a different sort than someone would use in revising a piece of writing.

Because every student in the class will have read all of the short stories for which covers are made, once the covers are completed, they should be posted conspicuously around the room. Each student in each group should write a paragraph explaining the group's depiction of the story. Ask students not in the group that created each cover to tell what part of the story each cover depicts. They should also identify the characters in the story. If the covers are done literally, interpretation should not be difficult. After interpretations have been offered, all students in the group should read their explanations aloud, defending them if they have to.

This activity helps students:

- depict character and situation in a different medium
- interpret someone else's depiction of character and situation
- develop the skills of supporting an argument

Visualizing—Part 2: Theme

The first visualizing activity had to do with literal interpretation and with plot (situation). This continuation focuses on the more difficult task of identifying and depicting theme.

The situation is the same as it was for the first part of the activity. The only difference is that this time the cover the students make will reveal the theme of the story. It will probably be much more figurative than literal.

For example, if one were doing a cover for Ernest Hemingway's *The Old Man and the Sea,* the result in Part 1 of the exercise might be a picture of the back of an old man in a small fishing boat straining to pull in a huge fish on the end of a taut line. A thematic depiction might be of the same old man, this time on land, walking away from a gutter in which the rotting skeleton of a huge fish is seen. His hands would tell the story. They would be held out in such a way as to ask, "What's the use?"

Once the drawings are done, the same process is followed as for the first version of the activity, but this time each student contributes to composing a single written explanation and justification of the group's depiction. Arriving collectively at a single statement helps them to learn how to incorporate diverse ideas differently expressed into a single, unified piece of writing.

As a follow-up, you might encourage students to bring to class covers of books they have read and to tell the class something about each book, showing how the cover, created by a professional designer, relates to the volume.

This activity helps students:

- distinguish between plot and theme
- distinguish between literal and figurative interpretation
- shape and defend an argument or explanation

Illustrating a Story or Novel

This activity can be used with practically any piece of literature that contains sharp characterization. For example, Homer's *Odyssey* or

Chaucer's *Canterbury Tales* work well, but so do selections from the Tilbury poems of Edwin Arlington Robinson or from Edgar Lee Master's *Spoon River Anthology.* Your students' job will be to create a visual universe based on literature.

Once the work of literature to be depicted has been decided upon, the division of labor takes place. The task is for groups of five or six students to create panels that depict scenes from the literary material. An overall planning session is crucial here, so to make the project proceed smoothly, each group should elect a spokesperson. A major task for the spokespersons will be to decide what needs to be depicted in order to present a fair view of all the literary material the students are working with.

Once each group knows what scenes it is responsible for, it begins to work with large rolls of butcher paper, first making rough sketches or cartoons on the paper, then working them into finished pieces. Some members of each group will serve as literary arbiters, making sure that their group's depiction is faithful to the details of the text.

When all of the panels have been completed, they should be affixed sequentially to the wall. Perhaps the work of another class can be affixed sequentially to the wall as well. Perhaps another class can be invited in to see the panels and to be told about what each depicts. This project might extend over several days.

This activity helps students:

- work collaboratively to interpret literature
- read carefully for detail that they will transmit into drawing
- converse effectively to coordinate their efforts

Treating the Theme of Revolution and Romanticism through Pop Art

At the beginning of a class, point out to students that the rock group U2 introduces the song "Sunday Bloody Sunday" (on the album *Under a Blood Red Sky*) with the disclaimer "This is not a rebel song." Ask them to listen to the song and see if they agree. Play the song. Conduct a class discussion about whether or not "Sunday Bloody Sunday" is a "rebel song." (Be sure the discussion includes some reference to the images of despair in the song. Does despair often breed rebelliousness, even revolution?)

Now ask students to listen to Sting's "Russia" from his album *The Dream of the Blue Turtles.* Ask them to determine whether this song suggests any hope for the future, despite ideological differences between the two superpowers (Russia and the U.S.) portrayed in the song. After the song has played, lead a class discussion on whether or not the song expresses hope. (Be sure students identify the "hysteria" referred to in the song's first line; also be sure they interpret the line "We share the same biology, regardless of ideology.")

Now show students the following cartoon. Conduct a class discussion about what the cartoonist might be trying to suggest. (Be sure that the terms *glasnost* and *perestroika* come up in the discussion, as well as the issue of Gorbachev's "revolutionary" leadership in the Soviet Union—indeed, in the world.)

Reprinted by permission: Tribune Media Services.

Ask students to read "Anthem for Doomed Youth," written by the young English soldier Wilfred Owen, who died in action just a week before Armistice Day, 1918. Before they read the poem, ask them to determine whether it is a patriotic poem or a protest poem. (Resist defining those terms for students; rather, ask them to interpret the poem according to their own concepts of patriotism and protest.)

Anthem for Doomed Youth

What passing-bells for these who die as cattle?
– Only the monstrous anger of the guns.
Only the stuttering rifles' rapid rattle
Can patter out their hasty orisons.
No mockeries now for them; no prayers nor bells,
Nor any voice of mourning save the choirs, –
The shrill, demented choirs of wailing shells;
And bugles calling for them from sad shires.

What candles may be held to speed them all?
Not in the hands of boys, but in their eyes
Shall shine the holy glimmers of goodbyes.
The pallor of girls' brows shall be their pall;
Their flowers the tenderness of patient minds,
And each slow dusk a drawing-down of blinds.

Finally, divide students into small groups. Tell each group to discuss the poem and decide whether it is a patriotic poem or a protest poem. Each group must then choose one of two ways to represent the poem through another art form—they can either create a cartoon (something like the one they were shown earlier) or compose a song (something like the ones by U2 and Sting). After the projects are complete, each group can choose how it wishes to present its work to the class as a whole. (Perhaps the cartoons might be displayed and discussed, or the songs might be performed.)

This activity helps students:

- acquire skill in decision making and problem solving
- practice inferential and interpretive thinking processes
- cultivate inventive thinking by representing one art form in terms of another

From Poems to Cartoons

Select some entertaining or amusing poems from an anthology your students are using. Assign each student one poem to read aloud before the class. (Some students may wish to memorize their poems, which will be short ones, but this should not be a condition of the assignment.) Ask your students to follow the poems in their books and to "keep score," ranking the poems they like best and the ones they like least.

After about fifteen poems have been read, take a poll to determine which poems are most popular. The ones receiving the highest number of votes will constitute the poems on which each group of five or six students will work. Each group's task will be to create a comic strip of the poem, trying to depict such characteristics as setting, tone, characterization, and literal or figurative meaning. The groups consider how to achieve characterization by using language as a significant element in shaping character. Some will probably make effective use of talking animals in some of their illustrations.

Each group reports orally on the problems they had in depicting their poems accurately. What did they have to leave out? What compromises did they have to make? What was not available to them in their art medium that was available to the artist working with words? What was not available to the artist working with words that was available to them?

This activity helps students:

- understand how artists transform ideas into verbal images
- understand how verbal images are transformed into graphic images
- assess the differences and similarities among various art forms

Setting Poems to Music

This activity can be done by individuals or groups. Assign students about a dozen short poems, preferably ones like Emily Dickinson's "A Narrow Fellow in the Grass" or "There's a Certain Slant of Light" that are compact but loaded with visual imagery. Once students have read the poems, their assignment is to go through their family albums or to find pictures from other sources that might be used to illustrate one of the poems they have read. They should also try to find some modern music into which the words of the poem might be inserted, possibly making a cassette to reflect this effort.

Either individually or collectively, students copy the poem on colored construction paper, trying to use paper and colors that reveal something about the poem. They then illustrate their poems by attaching pictures to the sheets of construction paper. Display the poem/picture combinations in some way. Set a day aside so that each student (or group) who has made a cassette can play it and each student (or group) who has prepared a musical arrangement can perform it.

This activity helps students:

- realize that poetry has musicality
- understand that poetry succeeds through the images it creates
- discover that poetry is related to objects in the world around them

Making Visual Poems

Not all poems are created by writing words across a page in straight lines. Visual poems incorporate words and forms into statements that are both poetic and visual. For example, some students will have seen the poem that depicts the adage about finding a needle in a haystack. The haystack consists of the word *haystack* written over and over, parts of it sticking out of the mound like straws in a real haystack. Somewhere within this word construction is a single word other than *haystack.* It is *needle,* and it is placed inconspicuously within the construction. Another example is Figure 3, which depicts a slogan currently popular among English teachers.

Students may work singly, in pairs, or in groups on this activity, which is to take an adage and create from it a visual image comprised of words that illustrate the adage. You might suggest such adages as "Let sleeping dogs lie," "A stitch in time saves nine," "What goes around comes around," and "Handsome is as handsome does," although students should be encouraged to supply their own.

Once students have completed these visual poems, display them around the room. Also, encourage students to copy them onto ditto

CURRICULUMCURRICULUMCURRICULUMCURRI
CULUMCURRICULUMCURRICULUMCURRICULUM
CURRICULUMCURRICULUMCURRICULUMCURRI
CULUMCURRICULUMCURRICULUMCURRICULUM
CURRICULUMCURRICULUMCURRICULUMCURRI
CULUMCURRICULUMCURRICULUMCURRICULUM
CURRICULUMCURRICULUMCURRICULUMCURRI
CULUMCURRICULUMCURRICULUMCURRICULUM
CURRICULUMCURRICULUMCURRICULUMCURRI
CULUMCURRICULUMCURRICULUMCURRICULUM
CURRICULUMCURRICULUMCURRICULUMCURRI
CULUMCURRICULUMCURRICULUMCURRICULUM
CURRICULUMCURRICULUMCURRICULUMCURRI
CULUMCURRICULUMCURRICULUMCURRICULUM
ULUM
CURRICULUM
CURRICULUM

writing

Figure 3. A literal representation of the slogan "writing-across-the-curriculum."

masters or photocopy them in sufficient quantity to make a poetry booklet for each student in class.

This activity helps students:

- think divergently
- analyze what some sayings they have always taken for granted might really mean
- engage in wordplay that captures the pleasure of poetry

Writing

Writing activities here that employ the arts include prewriting and revision.

Prewriting

Writing is arguably the most complex language art because it requires us to *produce* language—not merely by uttering words, which is ephemeral, but by *representing* words on paper, which gives at least the illusion of permanence. Writing, therefore, seems more formal than speech and can be an intimidating activity for students—hence, the pedagogical importance of *prewriting* (what we do to get ready to write). The other arts can become a fertile source for helping students both want to write and find something to say.

The "Harris Burdick" Approach to Story Writing

Chris Van Allsburg, who compiled a picture book called *The Mysteries of Harris Burdick,* writes in the introduction to that book about Harris Burdick's identity. It seems that Mr. Burdick had written and illustrated fourteen stories, which he was interested in getting published. After visiting with a prospective publisher one day, he left his fourteen drawings (minus the actual stories) for an editor to review. He promised to return the next day, but he was never seen or heard from again. Allsburg's book is the first published appearance of Burdick's drawings. The stories themselves have never been discovered.

Tell students about Harris Burdick. If possible, show them the fourteen pictures from Allsburg's book, each of which has an accompanying title and caption composed by Burdick himself. The titles and captions are intended to make the pictures mysterious. For example, one drawing shows two children standing on a stony shore, throwing rocks into the water. The title is "A Strange Day in July," and the caption reads, "He threw with all his might, but the third stone came skipping back" (pp. 9–10). Another shows a young girl standing in a forest, looking sadly at two objects in the palm of her hand. The title is "Oscar and Alphonse," and the caption says, "She knew it was time to send them back. The caterpillars softly wiggled in her hand, spelling out 'goodbye' " (pp. 29–30).

This book suggests many potentially useful ideas for prewriting. One might be to have students create pictures with intriguing titles and captions, just as Harris Burdick did. (An option for some students who have a legitimate case of "drawer's block" is to cut out and bring to class pictures they locate in some source. They must, however, create original titles and captions for the pictures.) Then, working together in groups of three to five, each student selects a picture, title, and caption that he or she will develop into a full-blown story. (Students may select their own pictures or someone else's.) After the students have created their first-draft stories, they go back into their small groups for round-robin reading, followed by suggestions for possible revisions. Final-draft stories may be read aloud on a voluntary basis. All stories may be displayed in the classroom.

This activity helps students:

- practice imaginative thinking
- draw inferences from visual stimuli
- invent material for story writing

Using Art to Create a Mood for Prewriting

For this lesson, an artwork—a painting, a photograph, a piece of statuary, or some other construction—is necessary. The piece of art has to be large enough for everyone in the room to see it easily and in detail. Ideally, the work selected should be unfamiliar to everyone in the class.

You will need to prepare students specifically for this lesson the day before it is to occur. They should think of the lesson as providing them with a special opportunity, although a quite different one from what most of them have been used to.

If possible, darken the room before students enter. Warn them the day before to expect this. As they enter the class, music should be playing, preferably something they are not familiar with but that captures the tone of the art object on display as closely as it can. The art object should be lighted with a simple spotlight or some other illumination that can be focused upon it.

All that happens for the first ten or fifteen minutes is that you and the students sit quietly, looking deeply at the piece of art on display. The music should keep the room from being utterly silent, a condition that many students find difficult. Finally, when the time seems right, make a remark about the piece of art, but not an obvious observation of something that can be verified. Avoid such questions as "How many buildings do you see in the picture?" or "What constitutes the picture's center of interest?" or "How would you describe the old man's expression?"

Rather, you might set the tone of the discussion by making an affirmative statement, something like "The dark sky reminds me of the old man's mood" or "He is clutching the child's hand as though he doesn't expect to see her again" or "The arching trees look as though they are protecting the revelers." Then say, "What does the picture say to you? What do you notice most about it?" The most important question toward which you are working is "How does the picture make you feel?" All of the other questions and comments should lead up to this essential question.

Once you ask this question and once a number of students have responded to it, turn on the lights and encourage the students to write freely on something like "What are your feelings at this moment?" (Write along with your students.) The drafts should be shared the next day by having people volunteer to read aloud what they have written.

Long lapses of silence are to be expected in this activity. There could be some giggling, although playing the music softly and preparing students for the exercise the day before should minimize this risk. Not all students can handle an exercise as sedentary and introspective as this one. If you plan to use it, let your students know that it affords them a special opportunity that requires maturity on their part, and that you are exposing them to it because you think they have the maturity to benefit from it.

This activity helps students:

- look beyond the surface of a work of art and analyze it deeply
- react to a work of art in a personal, nonthreatening way and write about that reaction
- imbibe a mood and later reflect that mood in a piece of informal writing

Using Film and Print to Teach Comparison and Contrast

At the beginning of a week, ask students to read a short story from their literature anthologies. (For this activity, choose the same short story for all to read.) In advance of their reading, tell students you would like them to choose a scene from the story and rewrite it as if they were Hollywood screenwriters, i.e., using only stage directions and dialogue. Tell them they should complete their drafts by Thursday.

On Thursday and Friday, divide students into groups of three and ask them to share their screenplays with one another, with group members taking speaking parts for each screenplay they share. After each student's screenplay has been "performed" within the group, ask each group to select someone to serve as recorder. Each group will discuss what film can do better than print, and vice versa, with recorders making notes of what group members say. Hold a "debriefing" session with the whole class, in which recorders serve as spokespersons for their respective groups. Write on the chalkboard your selected responses from recorders. (Two sample points: film can rely upon visual images and color to create setting and mood, while print must rely upon words; print can let us know what unspoken thoughts are in the minds of characters better than film can. While these two points of comparison perhaps show the superiority of one medium over another, each medium can benefit from trying to accomplish what the other naturally does better.)

As a "term" assignment (perhaps for a grading period or a full semester), ask students to read a novel and then see a film based upon the novel. Afterwards, they must write comparison/contrast pieces that point out the similarities and differences between the novel's treatment of setting, plot, character, and theme and the film's treatment of those elements. (Students might choose to pool their resources and rent films from video stores. This approach would enable them to return to various scenes of films for further viewing and analyzing.) Some students might ask for suggestions. You might recommend the following: *The Chocolate War* by Robert Cormier and *The Outsiders* by S. E. Hinton (two contemporary adolescent novels made into films); Anne Tyler's *The Accidental Tourist* and Bernard Malamud's *The Natural* (these novels have more mature themes). And, of course, you might recommend some "classics" that are available in film rental stores, like *Wuthering Heights, The Red Badge of Courage, The Grapes of Wrath,* and so on.

This activity helps students:

- perceive similarities and differences between film and print as media for artistic expression
- deepen their understanding of the elements of fiction

- differentiate the assets and limitations of both print and nonprint art forms

Revision

While prewriting deals with what we do to get ready to write, revision deals with what we do to improve earlier drafts. Helping students become effective revisers of their writing is a long and difficult process. The other arts can help.

Using Sketches to Teach Revision

Catherine Golden (1986) has written about how she used J. D. Ingres's sketches for the *Portrait of the Comtesse d'Haussonville* to help students see the value of revising, as well as develop some of the skills necessary to become effective revisers. She showed students that "the way in which a painter moves from sketch to completed painting . . . serve(s) as an analogue for a way of progressing from draft to final paper" (p. 59). She did this by bringing to class three slides that show pencil-and-crayon "drafts" of Ingres's *Portrait,* plus a copy of the final painting itself. (She discovered the slides in the University of Michigan's art history library.) As Golden's students looked at the slides, they observed that the first two show the woman's face growing more defined; they also noted that the artist added, deleted, and otherwise changed various aspects of his "drafts" to create a focus for the final painting. The major point Golden makes, however, is this: her students observed through their analyses of Ingres's sketches that any change in a composition (be it a sketch or a piece of writing) can affect the symmetry of the whole—*revision, therefore, must always be done with an eye on the whole piece rather than merely its individual parts.*

If possible, find the sketches that Golden used and show them to your class. (Perhaps you might locate others.) Short of that, ask the art teacher to identify students who might have some "draft" sketches available for use in your class. If none are available, perhaps some art students could be persuaded to produce a series of draft sketches just for your particular use.

By showing students that a "final-draft" painting evolves from a series of sketches, you can emphasize the importance and even enhance students' understanding of the process of revision. You might show students a "first-draft" sketch and ask them to describe what they see. (In a first-draft sketch, the artist is trying to capture an initial vision of the piece.) With subsequent sketches, ask students to comment on the changes they see, emphasizing how each change affects their view of the whole. After analyzing the sketches, help students make comparisons to drafting a written composition. In particular, help them to see that revision is an organic process of evolution. Revision helps a writer move from an initial vision (first draft), through changes in the vision, to a fully conceptualized, unified representation of the vision (final draft). The use of "first-draft" sketches can help students perceive revision in this way. The goal, of course, is to help students in their own writing to produce final drafts that are more unified and ultimately more effective than their previous drafts.

This activity helps students:

- increase their powers of observation
- practice analytical thinking
- deepen their understanding of the revision process

Using Songs to Teach Audience Awareness in the Revision Process

Invite students to bring to class recordings of the same song sung by two or more different people. Help them see that many artists—especially popular singers and bands—tailor their styles to their audiences. Mahalia Jackson or Pearl Bailey, for example, would probably sing "When the Saints Go Marching In" one way at a friend's funeral and another way at a civil rights rally on the Washington Monument Mall. In doing so, the singer acknowledges her understanding of what is appropriate to specific occasions and audiences. She also acknowledges that the same words can mean different things in different situations and settings, and she revises her presentation accordingly.

People do the same thing dozens of times every day. We all adjust our language and level of usage to our audiences, talking quite differently to the pet dachshund who has just eaten our shoe than to our three-year-old neighbor who smiles across the driveway at us, and quite differently to our teachers than to either the dachshund or the three-year-old neighbor.

Have your students play several recordings that show how different artists present the same song. Encourage them to discuss the differences they detect in each presentation, indicating how the tone and style of the song differ in each case and speculating on what makes the difference and on what sort of audience each artist seems to be trying to reach. (This part of the activity should take about twenty-five minutes.)

Now ask each student to write one paragraph on an assigned topic, having each writer stipulate the audience (e.g., parents, teachers, peers) for which the paragraph is intended. Some of the following topics might work well for many student writers:

> Our twenty-seven-minute lunch period is too short.
>
> Teachers should (should not) accept late assignments without penalty.
>
> Students' grades should (should not) be reduced for irregular attendance.
>
> Assignments outside the English class should (should not) be down-graded for writing deficiencies.
>
> Students should (should not) be allowed to leave the school building and grounds when they have free periods.

At the end of the hour, collect all papers. The next day, redistribute them so that no student has his or her own draft, making sure that student A has student B's paper and vice versa. Allow students about twenty-five minutes to revise the papers they have received for a clearly identified audience different from that chosen by the original writer. Remind them of how singers adjust their styles to different audiences and situations.

At the end of the twenty-five minutes, have each student pair off with the person who has his or her paper, and have them read each other's revision, then discuss the kinds of changes that each reviser has made and why each made these revisions. They should discuss also how effective and appropriate each piece of writing is in communicating with the audience the writer has identified.

This activity helps students:

- identify and write to specific audiences
- evaluate each other's writing for its appropriateness to a specific audience
- gain an ability to control tone and style in order to accommodate a variety of audiences

Bibliography

Ausubel, David P. 1968. *Educational Psychology: A Cognitive View.* New York: Holt, Rinehart, and Winston.

Barnet, Sylvan. 1985. *A Short Guide to Writing about Art.* Boston: Little, Brown and Company.

Barnett, Lincoln. 1964. *The Treasures of Our Tongue: The Story of English from Its Obscure Beginnings to Its Present Eminence as the Most Widely Spoken Language.* New York: Knopf.

Baron, Dennis E. 1982. *Grammar and Good Taste: Reforming the American Language.* New Haven: Yale University Press.

Barrie, John. 1986. "G. H. Bantock's Conceptualization of the Relationship between the Expressive Arts and Education." *Journal of Aesthetic Education* 20(2): 41–50.

Barzun, Jacques. 1986. *A Word or Two Before You Go.* Middletown, Conn.: Wesleyan University Press.

Berthoff, Ann. 1981. *The Making of Meaning.* Montclair, N.J.: Boynton/Cook.

Breen, Jennifer, ed. 1988. *Wilfred Owen: Selected Poetry and Prose.* London: Routledge.

Britton, James, et al. 1975. *The Development of Writing Abilities (11–18).* London: Macmillan Education Ltd.

Bruner, J. S. 1966. "Language as an Instrument of Thought." In *Problems in Language and Learning,* edited by A. Davis. London: Heinemann.

———. 1969. *On Knowing: Essays for the Left Hand.* Cambridge: Harvard University Press.

———, et al. 1966. *Studies in Cognitive Growth.* New York: John Wiley.

Claiborne, Robert. 1983. *Our Marvelous Native Tongue: The Life and Times of the English Language.* New York: New York Times Books.

Cussler, Elizabeth B. 1989. "Art in the Literature Class." *English Journal* 78(3): 28–31.

deBono, Edward. 1976. *Teaching Thinking.* London: Penguin Books.

DeLong, Patrick D. 1965. *Art in the Humanities.* Englewood Cliffs, N.J.: Prentice-Hall.

Dewey, John. 1931. *Art as Experience.* New York: Capricorn Books.

Edwards, Betty. 1979. *Drawing on the Right Side of the Brain.* Los Angeles: Jeremy P. Tarcher.

Emig, Janet. 1978. "Hand, Eye, Brain: Some Basics in the Writing Process." In *Research on Composing,* edited by Charles R. Cooper and Lee Odell. Urbana, Ill.: National Council of Teachers of English.

Fleming, William. 1986. *Arts and Ideas.* 7th ed. New York: Holt, Rinehart and Winston.

Fulwiler, Toby. 1982. "The Personal Connection: Journal Writing across the Curriculum." In *Language Connections: Writing and Reading across the Curriculum,* edited by Toby Fulwiler and Art Young. Urbana, Ill.: National Council of Teachers of English.

Gardner, Helen. 1970. *Art through the Ages.* 5th ed. Revised by Horst de la Croix and Richard G. Tansey. New York: Harcourt, Brace and World.

Gardner, Howard. 1973. *The Arts and Human Development.* New York: John Wiley and Sons.

Golden, Catherine. 1986. "Composition: Writing and the Visual Arts." *Journal of Aesthetic Education* 20(3): 59–68.

Hayakawa, S. I. 1941. *Language in Thought and Action.* New York: Harcourt Brace Jovanovich.

Johnson, Ron, and Jan Boone. 1976. *Understanding the Film.* Skokie, Ill.: National Textbook Company.

Joos, Martin. 1961. *The Five Clocks.* New York: Harcourt Brace Jovanovich.

Kelly, G. 1955. *The Psychology of Personal Constructs.* New York: Norton.

May, Rollo. 1975. *The Courage to Create.* New York: Bantam Books.

McCrum, Robert, William Cram, and Robert McNeil. 1986. *The Story of English.* New York: Viking.

McNeese, Tim. 1986. "Raiders of the Lost Art: Using the 'Painted Word' in Writing." *English Journal* 78(3): 34–37.

Moffett, James. 1968. *Teaching the Universe of Discourse.* Boston: Houghton Mifflin.

Ornstein, Robert. 1972. *The Psychology of Consciousness.* San Francisco: W. H. Freeman.

Pei, Mario. 1973. *Double-Speak in America.* New York: Hawthorn Books.

———. 1978. *Weasel Words: The Art of Saying What You Don't Mean.* New York: Harper and Row.

Phillips, Leay. 1989. "First Impressions: Introducing Monet to Megadeth." *English Journal* 78(3): 31–34.

Polanyi, Michael. 1967. *The Tacit Dimension.* Garden City, N.Y.: Anchor Books, Doubleday.

Postman, Neil, Charles Weingartner, and Terence P. Moran, eds. 1969. *Language in America.* New York: Pegasus.

Read, Herbert. 1937. *Art and Society.* New York: Macmillan.

Rico, Gabriele L. 1989. "Daedalus and Icarus Within: The Literature/Art/ Writing Connection." *English Journal* 78(3): 14–24.

Rosenblatt, Louise M. 1986. "The Aesthetic Transaction." *Journal of Aesthetic Education* 20(4): 122–28.

Smith, Frank. 1971. *Understanding Reading.* New York: Holt, Rinehart and Winston.

———. 1973. *Psycholinguistics and Reading.* New York: Holt, Rinehart and Winston.

Sorel, Nancy Caldwell. 1970. *Word People.* New York: American Heritage Press.

Squire, James. 1983. "Composing and Comprehending: Two Sides of the Same Basic Process." *Language Arts* 60: 581–89.

Thomas, Lewis. 1978. *The Lives of a Cell.* New York: Penguin Books.

Van Allsburg, Chris, ed. 1984. *The Mysteries of Harris Burdick.* Boston: Houghton Mifflin.

Vonnegut, Kurt. 1987. *Bluebeard.* New York: Dell Publishing.

Vygotsky, Lev. 1962. *Thought and Language.* Translated by E. Hanfmann and G. Vakar. Cambridge: MIT Press.

Wolfe, Denny, and Robert Reising. 1983. *Writing for Learning in the Content Areas.* Portland, Maine: J. Weston Walch.

Authors

R. Baird Shuman is professor of English, the English Department's director of development, and acting director of the Center for the Study of Writing at the University of Illinois, Urbana-Champaign. He has taught in the public schools of Philadelphia, at the University of Pennsylvania, San Jose State University, and Duke University. A visiting professor at the Moore Institute of Art, the Philadelphia Conservatory of Music, the Bread Loaf School of English, King Faisal University (Saudi Arabia), and the University of Tennessee at Knoxville, he has published critical studies of Clifford Odets, Robert E. Sherwood, and William Inge. He is author of *The First R: Fundamentals of Initial Reading Instruction; Strategies in Teaching Reading: Secondary; Classroom Encounters;* and other books. He has edited *Creative Approaches to Teaching English: Secondary; English in the 80's; Nine Black Poets; A Galaxy of Black Writing; Educational Drama for Today's Schools;* and *Questions Teachers Ask.* Professor Shuman is executive editor of *The Clearing House.*

Denny Wolfe is professor of English education, director of the Tidewater Virginia Writing Project, and associate dean in the Darden College of Education at Old Dominion University, Norfolk, Virginia. As an English teacher in secondary schools, he taught English, drama, speech, and journalism in grades 9 through 12. He also served as director of the Division of Languages for the North Carolina State Department of Public Instruction. Currently, he teaches courses in methods of teaching English and in language across the curriculum on both the undergraduate and graduate levels. Professor Wolfe served as chair of NCTE's Standing Committee on Teacher Preparation and Certification, which prepared the Council's *Guidelines for the Preparation of Teachers of English Language Arts* (1986). He has published over sixty articles on various aspects of teaching English, as well as two books, *Writing for Learning in the Content Areas* (coauthor) and *Making the Grade: Evaluating and Judging Student Writing.*